METUSELA ALBERT

THE 24
FALSE TEACHINGS
OF THE SDA CHURCH.

To order additional copies of this book, contact:
Xlibris
844-714-8691
www.Xlibris.com
Orders@Xlibris.com

ISBN: Softcover   979-8-3694-3184-9
          EBook   979-8-3694-3183-2

Print information available on the last page

Rev. date: 10/10/2024

Contents

GENESIS 1:1

Moses wrote, "In the beginning <u>God</u> created the heaven and the earth". (KJV).

SCRIPTURE READING - Isaiah 43:10-11 – (KJV).

GOD SAID TO PROPHET ISAIAH,

[10] "Ye are My witnesses," saith the Lord, "and My servant whom I have chosen, that ye may know and believe Me, and understand that I am He. <u>Before Me there was no God formed, neither shall there be after Me.</u>

[11] I, even I, am the Lord, and <u>besides Me there is no savior</u>".

....
....
....
....

SCRIPTURE READING - Isaiah 43:15 – (KJV).

GOD SAID TO PROPHET ISAIAH,

[15] I am the Lord, your Holy One, <u>the Creator</u> of Israel, your King".

....
....
....
....

NOTE: THE GOD OF PROPHET ISAIAH WAS THE CREATOR OF HEAVEN AND EARTH. THERE WAS NO GOD BEFORE HIM AND AFTER HIM. THEREFORE, THE GOD OF THE CHILDREN OF ISRAEL WAS NOT A TRINITY GOD. HE WAS JESUS.

....
....
....
....

NOTE: It is very IMPORTANT that you take time to read the Scripture Reading given above, and understand that there was only one GOD that existed in heaven. In fact, the GOD who created heaven and earth, was the same GOD who spoke to Prophet Isaiah, and HE was the I THE ALPHA AND OMEGA, who spoke to John the Revelator, on the Island of Patmos.

....
....
....
....

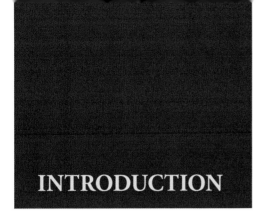

INTRODUCTION

Dear Reader,

The <u>main key</u> to recognize the false doctrines of the SDA Church, is to learn the truth about <u>who JESUS was</u>, in the Old Testament. Once you come to a good understanding that <u>JESUS was the ELOHIM who created heaven and earth</u>, then you can easily notice the false doctrines without any struggle. It is that simple.

NOTE: Chapters 2, 3, 4, 5, 6, and 7, were designed to help you understand who JESUS was, before His Incarnation into human flesh, through Mary at Bethlehem.

I am not writing about one or two false teachings by the SDA Church. I am informing you that there are <u>over 20 false teachings</u> by the SDA Church. So, stay tuned to learn the truth that perhaps many of you still have not learned yet. If you are an SDA member, then it is obvious that you still lack the knowledge of truth; and that is the reason you did not know of the 24 False Teachings within the SDA Church.

Like Judaism, the SDA Church was correct in believing that the Sabbath day is the seventh day of the week, which is SATURDAY. Most Protestant Churches observe Sunday as the Sabbath day; and they are already wrong.

However, if you are <u>not</u> an SDA member, then pay attention because you may be believing some of the false teachings by the SDA Church, that I am going to reveal. This Book is to provoke your mind to analyze your doctrines well.

As a former member of the SDA Church, I used to believe those false doctrines, but <u>not</u> anymore. Because I don't believe them anymore; so, what? Shall I keep quite and not let others know the subtle errors? Of course, not. Please don't get angry with me. Don't get offended. Be grateful to GOD who allowed you to come across this Book, so that you can become more informed about JESUS; and to realize the subtle errors. Give GOD the glory for allowing you to see those subtle false teachings, you are about to read.

The TEN CHAPTERS of <u>this Book</u> were designed for you to see the truth about JESUS. Once you realize that JESUS alone was the only GOD of Abraham, then you can easily notice the False Teachings by the SDA Church, OR by any other Church.

Without understanding who JESUS was, in the Old Testament, you will <u>not</u> be able to recognize the false teachings.

After having said that, let us begin our search.

. . . .
. . . .
. . . .
. . . .

A BRIEF HISTORY OF THE SDA CHURCH.

Around early 1840's, Mr. William Miller, a Baptist Preacher in America, was preaching the return of JESUS, will be on October 22, 1844 A.D. His Second Coming Theory was taken from Daniel 8:13-14. It is the 2,300 Days Prophecy which started on 457 B.C. and ended on October 22, 1844 A.D. A Great Religious Revival and Reformation took place back then.

A young lady by the name – Miss <u>Ellen G. Harmon</u>, and her family, became believers in Mr. William Miller's messages. However, when JESUS did <u>not</u> return, there was a Great Disappointment amongst the Advent Believers.

Miss Ellen G. Harmon was about 17 years of age during the Great Disappointment, in 1844 A.D. The main Group disintegrated to various groups. She later married Mr. White. She and her husband became part of the group called – Advent Believers. They still believed in the Advent of Christ. And later, they came to the knowledge of the Seventh day Sabbath, which is Saturday.

Prior to 1863 A.D., Mrs. Ellen G. White, was having dreams and visions about heaven; and she became a Prominent figure among the Seventh-day Advent Believers.

In April, 1863 A.D., Mrs. Ellen G. White, her husband, and some others, formed the Seventh-day Adventist Church. The Sanctuary with Two Apartments given by GOD to Moses in the wilderness journey from Egypt to Canaan, <u>became the foundational truth</u> for Mrs. Ellen G. White and the Seventh-day Adventist Church.

THAT IS WHY THE SANCTUARY SERVICE WITH TWO APARMTENTS, THE SABBATH, AND THE COMING OF JESUS, ARE KEY DOCTRINES IN THE FUNDAMENTAL BELIEFS OF THE SDA CHURCH.

She wrote, there were Three Living Beings that existed in heaven, before the angels were created – the Father, the Son, and the Holy Spirit. The SDA Church believed that she was a Prophetess of GOD, and they held strongly to her writings; and called her writings, the Spirit of Prophecy (SOP), as mentioned in Revelation 19:10.

In fact, the SDA Church misinterpreted Revelation 19:10.

The SDA Church did not know that "the Spirit of Prophecy", mentioned in Revelation 19:10, refers to the writings of the Prophets of the Old Testament.

That proves that the SDA Church LEADERSHIP still got to learn how to interpret Scripture, in the Context. They have misled over 27 Millions of people.

....
....
....
....

CHAPTER 2

JESUS WAS THE ELOHIM WHO CREATED HEAVEN AND EARTH.

Let's Read Genesis 1:1. (KJV).

"In the beginning <u>God</u> created the heaven and the earth".

....
....
....
....

WHO CREATED HEAVEN AND EARTH?

ANSWER: GOD.

....
....
....
....

NOTE: THE SON OF GOD DID NOT CREATE HEAVEN AND EARTH. DON'T FORGET THIS POINT.

....
....
....
....

TAKE NOTE OF <u>THESE THREE POINTS</u>, BELOW:

1. The Begotten Son of GOD <u>did not</u> create heaven and earth.
2. GOD did <u>not</u> have a Begotten Son, in heaven, at the time of Creation.
3. There was <u>no third person</u> called Holy Spirit, at the time of creation.

When you know the <u>truth</u>, you will easily know the error(s). But if you don't the truth, you will <u>not</u> know the error(s).

UNDERSTANDING THE THREE POINTS ABOVE, WILL HELP YOU RECOGNIZE THE ERRORS BY JOHN AND PAUL IN THE NEW TESTAMENT.

....
....
....
....

SO, WHAT IS THE TRUTH?

1. JESUS WAS THE <u>ELOHIM,</u> WHO CREATED HEAVEN AND EARTH.

Read – Genesis 1:1-31; 2:1-3; Isaiah 43:10-11, 15.

2. JESUS WAS THE GOD OF ABRAHAM.

Read – Genesis 12:1-3.

3. JESUS WAS THE I AM THAT I AM, WHO SPOKE TO MOSES, AT THE BURNING BUSH.

Read - Exodus 3:13-14; John 5:39, 46; 8:56-58.

4. JESUS WAS THE <u>ELOHIM,</u> THE FIRST AND THE LAST, WHO SPOKE TO PROPHET ISAIAH.

Read - Isaiah 44:6, 24; 43:10-11, 15.

5. JESUS WAS <u>THE ALPHA AND OMEGA,</u> WHO SPOKE TO JOHN, ON THE ISLAND OF PATMOS.

Read - Revelation 21:5-7.

6. JESUS WAS <u>NOT</u> A TRINITY GOD.

7. JESUS WAS <u>NOT</u> THE SON OF ALPHA AND OMEGA.

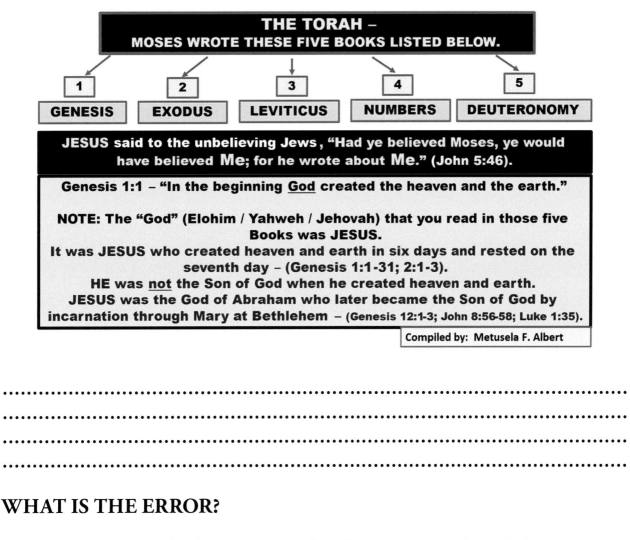

....
....
....
....

WHAT IS THE ERROR?

1. John 1:1-3 and John 3:16 *contradicted* Genesis 1:1 and Isaiah 43:10-11, 15.
2. Paul who wrote in Colossians 1:15-18 that JESUS was the <u>first-born</u> of all creatures, *contradicted* Genesis 1:1 and Isaiah 43:10-11, 15.
3. Paul and John *demoted* JESUS from being the EHOLIM who created heaven and earth, an everlasting GOD with no beginning and no ending; to someone with a beginning and an ending; a creature.

....
....
....
....

CHAPTER 3

JESUS WAS THE ELOHIM OF ABRAHAM, ISAAC, AND JACOB.

Read Genesis 12:1-3.

THE GOD OF ABRAHAM WAS NOT A TRINITY GOD.

- Genesis 12:1-3.(King James Version).

- 1. Now **the LORD** had said unto Abram, "Get thee out of thy country, and from thy kindred and from thy father's house, unto a land that I will show thee.

- ² And I will make of thee a great nation, and I will bless thee and make thy name great; and thou shalt be a blessing.

- ³ And I will bless them that bless thee, and curse him that curseth thee; and in thee shall all families of the earth be blessed."

DID YOU NOTICE THAT THE PRONOUN "I" WAS MENTIONED FOUR (4) TIMES? . . . . NOT "WE"

Compiled by: Metusela F. Albert

Read - Exodus 3:13-14. Further Reading - John 5:39, 46; 8:56-58.

JESUS WAS THE "I AM THAT I AM", WHO SPOKE TO MOSES, AT THE BURNING BUSH.

....

....

....

....

Please read <u>CHAPTER 2,</u> and understand it well before you precede any further. Thanks.

IMPORTANT POINT: When you have a good understanding of <u>CHAPTER 2</u>, you will find the rest of the Book, very easy to understand.

....

....

....

....

CHAPTER 4

ELOHIM TOOK HUMAN FLESH AND BECAME THE SON OF GOD, THROUGH MARY, AT BETHLEHEM.

Read Isaiah 43:10-11, 15.

Read John 5:39, 46; 8:56-58;

Luke 1:35; Matthew 1:21-23.

NOTE: Please go and read CHAPTER 2, and you will understand this CHAPTER.

....
....
....
....

CHAPTER 5

ELOHIM WAS NOT A TRINITY GOD, IN HEAVEN.

Since JESUS was the Creator of heaven and earth, the only Elohim of Abraham; therefore, HE was not a Trinity GOD, in heaven.

Please read CHAPTER 2 of this Book and understand it well. Once you have a good understanding of CHAPTER 2, the rest of the Book is very simple to understand.

I wrote these two Books to clarify the subject that JESUS was the only GOD, in heaven; and HE was not a TRINITY GOD.

You can purchase them online – www.xlibris.com and from other online Book Sellers.

The Book you are reading now is my 18TH BOOK. That means, you can find other Books I have written on other subjects, that may be of interest to you

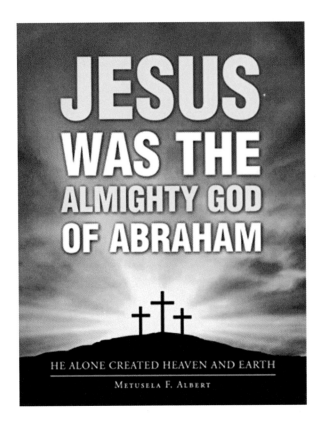

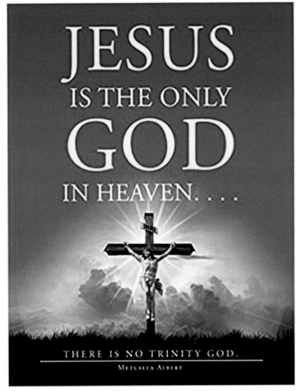

CHAPTER 6

ELOHIM DID NOT HAVE A BEGOTTEN SON, CALLED JESUS, IN HEAVEN.

The Creator of heaven and earth did not have a Begotten Son, called JESUS, in heaven.

Why?

Because, JESUS was the Creator of heaven and earth, who became the GOD of Abraham and the children of Israel. Did you get it? I hope so.

The GOD of Abraham did not have a Begotten Son, called JESUS, in heaven.

Once you understood that JESUS was the ELOHIM who created heaven and earth, who later became the GOD of Abraham, thus, you will not believe again in the False teaching that says, The GOD of Abraham had a Begotten Son, called JESUS, before the angels were created. It is that Simple.

WHAT ABOUT JOHN 3:16?

What was written in John 3:16, contradicted what GOD said in Genesis 1:1 and Isaiah 43:10-11.

When you fully understand that JESUS was the GOD who spoke to Prophet Isaiah, as recorded in Isaiah 43:10-11, it is clear that the GOD of the Prophets in the Old Testament era, did <u>not</u> have a Begotten Son, called – JESUS. It is that simple.

....
....
....
....

MY **12TH** BOOK WAS PUBLISHED ON SEPTEMBER 11, 2024.

YOU CAN PURCHASE ONLINE AT,

www.Xlibris.com

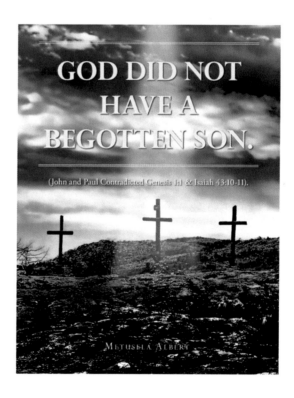

....
....
....
....

CHAPTER 7

JESUS IS THE <u>ONLY GOD</u>, SITTING ON THE THRONE, IN HEAVEN.

Read Revelation 4:1-11.

JESUS was the only One who came in human flesh, died at Calvary, resurrected, and ascended to heaven; and is living forever.

HE is the <u>only One</u> that is sitting on the THRONE, in heaven. Worship is due to Him, alone.

THERE IS <u>NO</u> TRINITY GOD SITTING ON THE THRONE, IN HEAVEN. WE SHOULD NOT WORSHIP A TRINITY GOD.

WORSHIPPING A TRINITY GOD, IS ANTI-CHRIST.

....
....
....
....

NOTE: THE SDA CHURCH STILL BELIEVES IN A TRINITY GOD.

....
....
....
....

CHAPTER 8

GOD'S CHURCH, IS NOT A DENOMINATION.

GOD'S Church are those who daily abide in JESUS CHRIST. They are <u>individuals</u> who love GOD and by faith, obey His law. GOD knows them. For example, the Patriarch Noah and his family, were members of GOD'S CHURCH, during the time of the flood.

Another example, the repentant thief on the Cross, was a member of GOD'S CHURCH. While on the Cross, JESUS assured him of eternal life when He returns the second time.

CHECK THIS OUT.

The SDA Church teaches that if you are <u>not</u> a baptized member of the SDA Church, you are not part of GOD'S remnant Church. Therefore, many people think that in order for them to become members of GOD'S REMANT CHURCH, they have to be baptized into the SDA Church. And if you left the SDA Church, you no longer a member of GOD'S REMNNAT CHURCH. In other words, you no longer got Salvation. This is Weird. This teaching is indirectly advocating - SALVATION BY THE SDA DENOMINATION.

My 13TH BOOK, I wrote, is attached.

....
....
....
....

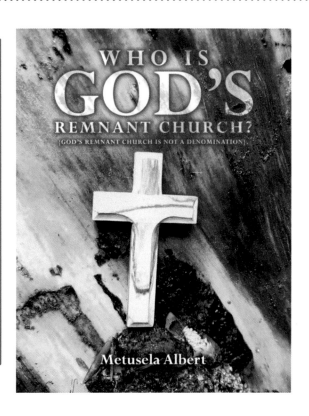

....
....
....
....

CHAPTER 9

MRS. ELLEN G. WHITE WAS NOT A PROPHETESS OF GOD.

THE TRUTH IS –

1. Mrs. Ellen G. White was <u>not </u>a Prophetess of GOD.
2. Mrs. Ellen G. White's writings are <u>not</u> the Spirit of Prophecy, mentioned in Revelation 19:10.
    The writings of the Old Testament Prophets, are the Spirit of Prophecy, mentioned in Revelation 19:10.

....
....
....
....

THE ERRORS BY MRS. ELLEN G. WHITE.

1. Mrs. White, wrote - "Christ was the Son of God; He had been one with Him before the angels were called into existence." SOURCE: <u>Patriarchs and Prophets</u>, page 38.

2. Mrs. Ellen G. White wrote in her Book – The Great Controversy, page 608, The Sabbath is the seal of GOD. (That is wrong).

3. Mrs. Ellen G. White wrote in her Book – The Great Controversy, about The Investigative Judgment that began in October 22, 1844 A.D. . . . (NOTE: That is unbiblical).

4. She wrote, "There are <u>three living persons</u> of the heavenly trio" . . . Book - Evangelism, page 615. (Wrong).

5. She wrote, "Christ, God's dear Son . . . He was One with the Father <u>before</u> the angels were created." - Book – The Story of Redemption, page 13. (THAT IS WRONG. She contradicted Isaiah 43:10-11).

THE FALSE TEACHING OF MRS. WHITE ABOUT JESUS.

- # 4 – Mrs. White, wrote. " Lucifer in heaven, before his rebellion, was a high and exalted angel, <u>next in honor to God's dear Son</u> . .
- Christ, God's dear Son, had the preeminence over all the angelic host. He was one with the Father before the angels were created . . . The great Creator assembled the heavenly host, that He might in the presence of all the angels confer special honor upon His Son.
- <u>The Son was seated on the throne with the Father,</u> and the heavenly throng of holy angels was gathered around them. The Father made known that it was ordained by Himself that Christ, His Son, should be equal with Himself, so that wherever was the presence of His Son, it was as His presence. The Word of the Son was to be obeyed as readily as the word of the Father. .. . Lucifer was envious and jealous of Jesus Christ."
- SOURCE: Story of Redemption, pages 13-14.

Compiled by: Metusela F. Albert.

....
....
....
....

PLEASE READ <u>THIS SLIDE BELOW</u> CAREFULLY, AND TAKE NOTE OF THE FALSE BELIEF <u>ABOUT THE FATHER AND JESUS</u>, BY MRS. ELLEN G. WHITE, IN HER BOOK – STORY OF REDEMPTION, PAGE 20.

THE FALSE TEACHING OF MRS. WHITE ABOUT THE FATHER AND JESUS.

- Mrs. White, wrote – "After the earth was created, and the beasts upon it, **the Father and the Son carried out their purpose**, which was designed before the fall of Satan, to make man in their own image. They had wrought together in the creation of the earth and every living thing upon it. And now **God said to His Son**, "Let us make man in our image."
- SOURCE: Story of Redemption, page 20.

Compiled by: Metusela F. Albert.

According to Ellen G White, it was the Father and the Son (Jesus), who created our planet earth and everything in it, including Adam and Eve. That is a <u>contradiction</u> of Genesis 1:1-31; 2:1-3.

In fact, Mrs. Ellen G. White <u>did not know</u> that JESUS was the GOD who created heaven and earth, who later became the GOD of Abraham. Furthermore, Mrs. Ellen G. White did <u>not</u> know that JESUS was the GOD called – <u>I AM THAT I AM</u>, who spoke to Moses at the Burning Bush- Exodus 3:13-14.

Did you notice? Mrs. Ellen G. White advocated that the Father and the Son (JESUS) were TWO DISTINCT BEINGS that existed before the Creation of Adam and Eve.

<u>CATCH THIS</u>: If Mrs. Ellen G. White was truly a Prophetess of GOD, then she should have known that JESUS was the ELOHIM who created our planet earth, including Adam and Eve. YEAH! GOD would have revealed it to her.

WARNING: For your information. Any Denomination that claims to be GOD'S true Church <u>with a Prophet</u>, and yet their Prophet did <u>not</u> know that JESUS was the Almighty GOD of Abraham, who created heaven and earth in six days, and <u>rested on the Seventh day</u>, is clear evidence that that particular Church is <u>another Fake Denomination</u>. Don't buy their lie. Stay away from that Denomination. Do I have to explain further? Did you not get it, yet? I hope you understand it. Thank you. GOD bless.

....

....

....

....

CHAPTER 10

THE 24 FALSE TEACHINGS
OF THE SDA CHURCH.

....
....
....
....

Please read carefully and note the distinctive wording of the points. Many of you who did not understand Isaiah 43:10-11 before, will find it hard to understand and differentiate the point. Hopefully, you can.

I tried my best to make the reader understand the truth from the error, in a simple way.

Don't let your preconceived mind block your reasoning power, to make you <u>not</u> understand. Thanks.

....
....
....
....

21

TWENTY–FOUR FALSE TEACHINGS OF THE SDA CHURCH.

1. THE SDA CHURCH WHICH STARTED IN 1863A.D., IS THE ONLY REMNANT CHURCH OF GOD.
2. GOD'S REMNANT CHURCH IS THE DENOMINATION CALLED   – THE SEVENTH DAY ADVENTIST CHURCH.
3. MRS. ELLEN G. WHITE IS GOD'S PROPHETESS.
4. THE WRITINGS OF ELLEN G. WHITE IS THE SPIRIT OF PROPHECY (SOP) MENTIONED IN REVELATION 19:10.
5. THE SABBATH IS GOD'S SEAL.
6. THE INVESTIGATIVE JUDGEMENT BEGAN ON OCTOBER 22, 1844, A.D.
7. JESUS WAS BORN TWICE. BORN IN HEAVEN BY THE FATHER AND BORN THE SECOND TIME BY MARY AT BETHLEHEM.
8. JESUS EXISTED WITH THE FATHER IN HEAVEN BEFORE THE ANGELS EXISTED.
9. JESUS WAS THE SON OF GOD IN HEAVEN WHO CREATED THE ANGELS.
10. JESUS WAS THE SON OF GOD WHO CREATED HEAVEN AND EARTH.
11. THE FATHER, THE SON, AND THE HOLY SPIRIT, ARE THREE DISTINCT PERSONS IN HEAVEN THAT MAKE UP ONE GOD.
12. JESUS HAD TO BE COMBINED WITH THE FATHER AND THE HOLY SPIRIT, TO MAKE ONE GOD.
13. THE HOLY SPIRIT IS THE THIRD PERSON, IN HEAVEN.
14. A TRINITY GOD IS SITTING ON THE THRONE, IN HEAVEN.
15. SIN IS INHERITED FROM ADAM AND EVE.
16. BABIES ARE BORN SINNERS DUE TO ADAM AND EVE'S SINS, WE INHERITED.
17. SIN IS BY THE SINFUL NATURE WE INHERITED FROM ADAM AND EVE.
18. IN ORDER TO BE A SINNER, ALL ONE HAS TO DO IS TO BE BORN.
19. ANYONE WHO IS NOT A BAPTIZED MEMBER OF THE SDA CHURCH, IS NOT PART OF GOD'S REMNANT CHURCH.
20. THREE IN ONE. . . . GOD THE FATHER + GOD THE SON (JESUS) + GOD THE HOLY SPIRIT = 1 GOD .
21. THE 144,000 IN REVELATION, IS A SYMBOLIC NUMBER.
22. SALVATION IS BY FAITH ALONE.
23. THE SANCTUARY IN HEAVEN HAS TWO APARTMENTS.
24. A TRINITY GOD IS SITTING ON THE THRONE, IN HEAVEN.

....
....
....
....

PUBLISHED ON AUGUST 20, 2024.

MY 10TH BOOK.

YOU CAN PURCHASE ONLINE AT – WWW.XLIBRIS.COM

METUSELA ALBERT

SALVATION IS CONDITIONAL.

....
....
....
....

MY 11TH BOOK-
WAS PUBLISHED IN
AUGUST 2024.

YOU CAN PURCHASE
ONLINE AT –
WWW.XLIBRIS.COM

....
....
....
....

PUBLISHED ON MARCH 04, 2011

PUBLISHED ON JUNE 01, 2021

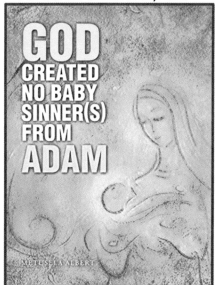

....
....
....
....

BOOK # 8

PUBLISHED ON MARCH 21, 2023.

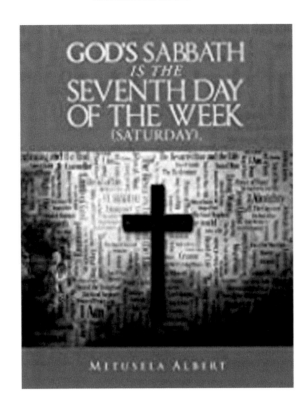

....
....
....
....

PUBLISHED ON AUGUST 17, 2021.

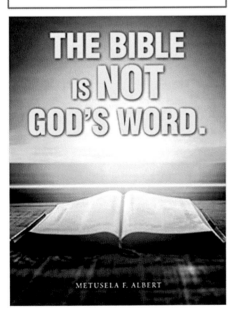

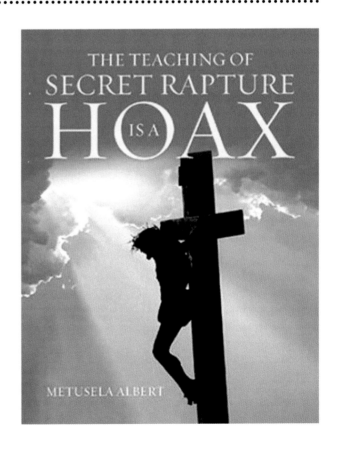

CONCLUSION

It is about time for the SDA members to evaluate their doctrines and follow the truth; and stop following a Denomination. They should discard the writings of Mrs. Ellen G. White, and read what GOD said to the Prophets in the Old Testament, about Himself. Stand up for JESUS; not for a Denomination called – Seventh-day Adventist Church nor for Ellen G White.

Abiding in JESUS CHRIST will make you a member of His Church. HE is coming to take the members of His Church. HE is not coming back to take a Denomination called SDA Church nor the members of the SDA Church. Belonging to the SDA Church will not make you a member of GOD'S CHURCH. While you become a member of the SDA Church, you are also believing in a TRINITY GOD; and that is against CHRIST. Did you not realize that? YOU cannot serve TWO MASTERS. Therefore, don't be afraid to condemn and rebuke the false teachings of the SDA Church.

- THE END -

Printed in the United States
by Baker & Taylor Publisher Services